Counting Eggs

Peter Daniels

*To Clodagh
Launch night
27 April 2012
with love from Peter*

Published 2012 by Mulfran Press
PO Box 812, Cardiff CF11 1PD
UK
www.mulfran.co.uk

The right of Peter Daniels to be identified as author
of this work has been asserted in accordance with the
Copyright, Designs and Patents Act, 1988.

Poems © Peter Daniels 2012

Cover design by John Fitzgerald Design [www.johnfitzgeralddesign.com].

ISBN 1-907327-15-5

All rights reserved. No part of this publication may be reproduced,
stored in a retrieval system, or transmitted at any time or by any
means, electronic, mechanical, photocopying, recording or otherwise
without the prior permission of the copyright holder, except in the
case of short extracts for inclusion in critical articles or reviews.

Printed by imprint**digital** in Devon [info@imprintdigital.net].

Little old man sits counting eggs.
Each time he counts, he's another egg short.
Don't give him sight of your gold, my friends.

Edith Södergran

Personal Acknowledgements

These poems are collected from more than twenty years of work, some having their origins before *Peacock Luggage*, the slim volume I shared with Moniza Alvi in 1992 from winning the Poetry Business Competition. Over the years, pamphlet publishers Janet Fisher, Peter Sansom, Richard Price, Leona Medlin and Helena Nelson have brought my poems into print, and previous potential collection manuscripts have been gone through by Carol Rumens, Jackie Kay, Michael Donaghy and Carl Morse. Mimi Khalvati has brought her indefatigable genius to shaping this version.

I would like to mention with gratitude my English teacher Tony Trott who encouraged my early efforts, and Kenneth King who got my poetry going at the end of my silent twenties. Of the many welcoming Americans, Phil Willkie deserves special mention as a generous host. My thanks also to fellow-Oscars Steve Anthony and Christina Dunhill, and to others too many to name who have helped with road-testing poems, in particular at the workshops hosted by Colin Falck, at Michael Donaghy's City University class and at the group that developed from it. Arvon and Poetry School courses are in there too, and the Sheffield Hallam MA with Sean O'Brien – even if I did stop writing afterwards for a few years. Graham Fawcett's translation workshops at the Poetry School woke up the words again, and a Hawthornden Fellowship allowed me to find Vladislav Khodasevich, sampled here but due soon to be published more fully by Angel Books.

James Grant has been my sturdy support and marketing man.

Previous publication:

"Shoreditch Orchid" won first prize in the Arvon Competition 2008, and the Ted Hughes prize for environmental poetry

"Wall Street": first published in *Art & Understanding* (Albany, NY)

"The Fireyard": first published in the Blinking Eye anthology

"Crossroads" and "February Charm": first published in *The Bow-wow Shop*

"Dull Funeral Home": first published in *Brangle*

"Excesses of the Prior of Inchcolm": first published in *Gairfish*

"Liverpool St": first published in the anthology *Gay Love Poetry* (Robinson)

"Breakfast, Palermo": first published in *The James White Review* (Minneapolis)

"Mall of Mammoths", "Mr Luczinski Takes a Tram" and "Tchotchkes": first published in *The North*

"The Monkey" (Khodasevich): first published in *PN Review*

"The Captive": commended in the *Poetry London* Competition 2011

"Nervous": first published in *The Rialto*

"Insects", "Fountain of Doom" and "Hunger": first published in *Scratch*

"Policeman, Stoke Newington" and "Mice": first published in *Southfields*

"Natural History Museum": first published in *Tabla*

"The Jar": first published in the *Times Literary Supplement*; "The Pump" won first prize in the *TLS* Poetry Competition 2010

"The Mormons in Sicily" and "Family": first published in *Verse* (St Andrews)

"Fountain of Arethusa, Syracuse": first published in *The Wide Skirt*

Pamphlets:

"Wall Street", "Breakfast, Palermo", "The Mormons in Sicily", "Excesses of the Prior of Inchcolm", "Kings", "Family" and "Hunger" in the Smith/Doorstop pamphlet *Be Prepared* (1994)

"Mice", "Wall Street", "Dull Funeral Home", and "Tchotchkes" in the Vennel Press pamphlet *Blue Mice* (1999)

"Heads", "The Jar", "Insects", "The Rainbow", "Mall of Mammoths", "Fountain of Arethusa, Syracuse", "Fountain of Doom", "Early", "Done", and "Housework" in the Smith/Doorstop pamphlet *Through the Bushes* (2000)

"Endeavours", "Done", "Liverpool St", and "Hunger" in the Mulfran Press pamphlet *Work and Food* (2010).

"The Pump", "Policeman, Stoke Newington", "Mr Luczinski Takes a Tram", "Nervous", "The Monkey of Forgetting" and "At the Forest Pool" in the HappenStance pamphlet *Mr Luczinski Makes a Move* (2011).

Contents

The Pump	1
The Jar	2
Mice	3
Insects	4
Knickerbockers	5
Flying	6
The Experts	7
Heads	8
The Rainbow	9
Mountain Ranges	10
Dull Funeral Home	11
Mall of Mammoths	12
Wall Street	14
The Fireyard	15
Cable Car	16
Breakfast, Palermo	17
Fountain of Arethusa, Syracuse	18
Persephone	19
The Mormons in Sicily	20
Discover London	21
Shoreditch Orchid	22
Policeman, Stoke Newington	24
Routemasters	25
Endeavours	26
Mr Luczinski Takes a Tram	27
The Monkey	28
Nervous	30

February Charm	31
The Special	32
City Boy	33
Found	34
The Monkey of Forgetting	36
The Captive	37
Natural History Museum	38
Outward	40
Excesses of the Prior of Inchcolm	42
At the Forest Pool	43
Fountain of Doom	44
Crossroads	45
In the Deep	46
Early	48
Vexation	49
Kings	50
Housework	51
Done	52
Therese	53
St Katharine's Dock	54
Tchotchkes	55
Family	56
Hunger	57
Liverpool St	58
Fragment 105a	59
Splendour	60
Birdsong	62
The Forge	63

The Pump

After piped water, the pump becomes redundant,
the handle chained down at the side: at rest, if you like.
The pump turns into "what we used to have",
but no one's minded to get rid of it.
With war declared they strip it down and oil it
in case Hitler bombs the reservoirs, but
water stays on tap. It's part of the yard,
with the paving in dark blue brick sluiced out
with a broom down to the drain.
A piece of ironwork painted green,
rusting into the wall, all of a piece.

It's what they call "the vernacular".
Flowers in tubs do brighten it up, the pump
redone in white, the name of the foundry and the date
picked out in black. It punctuates the composition,
sets off the door to the kitchen, the stone basin
where they used to put the bucket
planted up with nasturtiums that trail.
The place all spruce for the visitors,
now the redundant pump can stand for
all the strength it took the kitchen girl to crank it
and crank it till the steely water came up at last, and at last
she could find time to become somebody's grandmother.
Somebody look at the pump and think of her.

The Jar

Covered with raspberries bigger than any raspberries,
the vacuum-sealed lid is a hard lid to open,
but using knees and much clenching, in the end
I wrench it free – the vacuum goes *plock* – and something
brown and alive with legs comes up for its outing.

And it's enjoying the fresh air again, staggering
almost over the rim: fast as I can, I struggle
to put the lid back, not to deny it existed,
or kill it, but keep it there in the jar, alive
in its environment – whole raspberry preserve.

The manager opens it up, inspects the animal
sprawled over the soft meniscus of raspberry:
dead after all, killed by the shock of it probably.
But it's a carcass, sufficient to clinch the matter:
I go through to the aisle of jams to fetch another.

Mice

In the yellow water pail
two blue mice are floating.
They splashed through my sleep
last night, and I ignored them.

On the porch, three more mice
lie in the bottom of a dry pail,
withered, with a few old leaves,
and a scattering of droppings.

One mouse looks nibbled,
keeping the others alive
to chase the walls a while
inside the plastic drum.

How long before they died?
We could lie in wait and
count how many fall in:
but simpler to set some traps.

I throw the crisp mice out,
and this morning's two
wet and bloated ones,
with the water they drowned in,

scrape out the bucket of dried
mouseturds under the pump:
remember tonight
to keep the lid down on the water.

Insects

Insects, you know, have no
        genuine existence, not
as we mean it. Even as they
        crawl across your rug
they've got no personality,
        no understanding
– but they're so much
        less, even, than that.
Whilst they are of course
        supposed to be slimy inside
like us – and some of them
        do smell horrible, or make honey –
that's not what an insect
        really is or does. When
you look into it, you'll find
        it's all some plastic and metal
mechanical contrivance
        you'd never get the hang of,
though it might
        make some sense, if you could
get hold of the diagram.
        Hardware wholesalers
in Birmingham have
        big polypropylene
bins of them in racks.
        Women in Singapore
are going blind assembling them.
        I don't know why we should
put up with them at all.
        There's going to be no
getting away from them,
        not now they've been invented.

Knickerbockers

You young again, caught in a state and
knickerbockers of velvet: speech incoherent.

You told me: *It's the future, my new look.*
You welcomed in the new age, its inauguration.

A great wave of love came over me. I saw you
in pain yet above it, unbalanced, not ungraceful.

The breaking away, the scope of the impossible,
opening up your life of unguarded enquiry.

Standing there splendid in unashamed selfhood,
and this isn't all, you've worlds to incorporate.

A shadow remains, your smile like a scroll
on a granite sarcophagus, moss-encrusted.

You're more than your name, your undivided spirit
in space, but like a kite, riding at anchor.

Flying

My days are ready and I take them, flexible
and infinite, space for the filling.

Every moment I exercise my powers
and miraculously keep on flying.

Underneath, the crowd is ready to catch me,
their gasps open up like streamers and flags,

their oniony lunches, sweat and pheromones,
and acrid panic that spreads as it flickers.

I am for hire, as if they own me. I am like
their dust – nail filings or skin flakes.

I take my time. The old volcano opens
its ashy fumaroles, fiery and ready to fling.

Over the snowy mountain, I hover,
I dive and spread my folds as I'm falling.

The Experts

Spread out in the clouds like seagulls, they glide
and converge on you, they recognise your guilt.

Offer them your soul – they wouldn't care.
They slip past again, unhurried and glad.

Facing the sun, they swivel in one easy turn:
the moon they face is full, dead and cold.

They're the ones who do things you didn't know
how to imagine: disciplined and skilled.

Commuters on the escalators, working their passage.
The holy city cultivates their hearts of gold.

In your ridiculous clumsy habits, your needs
you can't express, you hop from clod to clod.

In your aspirations you hope for their blessings.
You are touched briefly as they pass by, sky-clad.

Heads

From the first there was no help but the sky
where the height above our heads went on and up
and where the signs came. The ground where the dew
soaked our feet, that was our own
because we lived there, though it might turn hard
or crumble, lose us in rising to mountains
or sink to the marshes and waters.
If we could ever find ourselves in clouds
our hearts would overbalance with that mastery.
Here we live, content under our hats, and a hat
protecting for the sake of heaven
won't help us fly, won't let us disappear.

The Rainbow

On board, the beasts were snorting in their stalls
with their hormones singing through the dung:
but by the hundred and fiftieth day
on the smooth waters in windless drizzle,
no one was ready any more. Noah lay relaxing
in a silk robe, unbuttoned, the Lord disapproving;
the brothers on deck betting on a sight of water nymphs,
monsters, any new thing at all.

And in the seventh month, the misty air was warm,
blanketing Ararat, and all of creation indoors
still steadily rolling, standing carefully
inside each other's smells; but then, wrong
footed, thrown when the bottom
bumped and scraped, sideways; a moment
of losing their places, a bout of questioning grunts.

The rutting began with a jumpy shivering,
the vocal flesh in a clamour for it all to subside,
to grant the abatement of waters, the planting of feet:
and the sun twisted through the cloud, turning
the sky; while the sky was shining back, to make
an example, a reason to feel now there would be more.

The whole tight ship had something to wait for.
Noah opened his window for the dove, which stood
a moment exercising claws and beak, before its wings clapped
and circled off, somewhere towards the faint mountains.

Mountain Ranges

after Wu Jiahua

Hills
embracing other hills

and

the uneven pathways
up to them

Dull Funeral Home
Wisconsin

A little past a car wash, on your left
a statue of a Holstein cow; on your right – "Hey,
can we stop the car a minute?" – it's that sign.

And whenever you need it, they have time.
Visit for a drink with the embalmer,
take as long as you like. Their expertise
is at your disposal.

Death needn't be a time to do anything.
If you want fuss, that's down to you.
This is America's Dairyland,
they put trust in cows, here. They know
your dead meat turns out as lively as your recipe.

Follow the standard procedures
for your denomination, hire the Fort Snelling
Memorial Chapel – "Staff available for weddings
and other pastoral acts". New Age
ritual consultancies advertise
"Planned observance for solemn
or festive occasions, parenting,
competitive events, establishing traditions,
anniversaries, pet loss".
                Whatever: but
if anything happens, ask for the Dull
Funeral Home. They don't need ideas.

Mall of Mammoths
Minneapolis, 1992

They've built the Mall of America
       on a prairie near the airport:
a hangar, to protect the world
       from the Minnesota climate.
The big everything – Bloomingdales
       to a blimp made of Lego:
leave the kids on flume rides and roller coasters.
        Get shopping.

Some of the shops are still discreetly unlet,
       given the recession.
One corner unit houses a sideshow
       of travelling Russians
bringing the Great Siberian Mammoths
       from that North to this,
with a support of stuffed wolverine, beaver,
       and three types of lemming.

The big attraction is
       the whole baby mammoth, who lost his mother.
Though his feet are still hairy,
       his body is now a dark brown leather
like my second-hand flying jacket
       with several additional sleeves,
laid out bulky but deflated,
       the breathing occupant missing.

Glass tanks of fluid contain
        his heart and his penis, on display:
that dead infant's plaything
        could incite grown men to envy.
Beside him, a full skeleton with twirling tusks,
        but not his mother;
and a skull – "Yes, you may touch!"
        – its features worn down to melting.

Back at the entrance,
        three Russian women in smocks
are selling lacquerwork nesting dolls
        and fairytale boxes;
enamel mammoth brooches –
        "I Am From Siberia" – and trays
full of remaindered Lenins.
        I am in America, and buying.

Wall Street

We walk further downtown, beyond the Village graffiti
that says AIDS IS THRUSH
AND IT'S CURABLE!
Life is money and the buildings are bigger here.
It's Ash Wednesday,
this is a day to commemorate
some crisis: all the last-born, maybe,
picked from among the perfect suits, the ones
wearing on their groomed brows a smudge
like a smear of sex. Look how ready they are,
it makes them hunger for six weeks without sin.

Being with my sacrilegious Manhattan friend,
it's time to look at a few spiky old churches,
because we don't visit here often.
Remarkable needlework: the white altarcloth
with crossed pairs of three-tail scourges in red.
More smudges: gladly humble
to wear this dirt mark in public.
And Jesus, with his robes hanging off him,
stands at a bank of candles, warming his hands.

The Fireyard

At the back, the last room, lucky to get it.
The whole hotel smells of damp curry,
facilities not special.

I settle down with the old t.v. showing Winter Olympics,
two rival skaters perform their separate circles
but I shift across to the local Chinese stations.
Men in suits all the same shade of grey,
seems to be the Taiwanese Parliament.

The spyhole lens in the door
is fitted the wrong way round
– hm? There's a label in my new
underpants – "Inspected by Carol" –
I stick it over.

Through the venetian blinds, outside
I spy the Fire Station yard, the men
idly shooting hoops, playing a hose on a car.
How many visitors must bless this
pent-up exercise. San Francisco
in its own bored heat, ready for flames.

Cable Car

Time for a cable car ride, back up to the top
where the streets are paved with diamonds,
to stop you sliding down again. I take it
to visit my friend Ed, in his old job
(this is years ago) selling books
at the cathedral on its height
blessing the city of fog and gold,
the quake-proofed buildings, the multitudes.
Someone has been working out some simultaneous
four-dimensional equations,
how to pay for it: and that's not allowing
for when the earth moves,
the mould busting itself
birthing the new order, now and then.
City of faith and freedom to follow the gleam
on the edge of its cliff.
Multiplication still leaves us one factor short:
the land we live on, and how we fit on it.
The streets go up like graphs
mapping their value, and the cost
of the paving. But we forget that,
held under the city's charm.
Let's all pile into
the cable car. The brakeman
leans over to the driver.
"Okay," he says. "Ding ding."

Breakfast, Palermo

One golden glazed bun, sliced open.
One scoop of custardy ice cream, speckled
with chips of fruit and chocolate.
Sandwich them lavishly.

To be eaten in uniform by a young soldier,
with one careless hand, espresso in the other.
At the chrome bar, more coffee is hissing.
Sunshine slants in early, yellow.
Not a speck on his trousers.

Fountain of Arethusa, Syracuse

At the Fountain of Arethusa:
spring-fed pool next to the inland sea,
where the goddess changed a frightened nymph
to a fresh pool on an island;

at the pool of the nymph, in a city of marble streets
and perpetual nonchalant motion,
a pool with circular walls of stone, pond plants and a swan,
I'm crossing the street with my sister, and for once
the traffic stops.

A woman is slowly crossing by the Fountain,
her red high heels perching on polished stone,
her tumbling pile of black hair floating, trembling;
she's crossing the street with her hips
in a tight red cone of a skirt,
and with her mouth
she's working on licking a deep strawberry ice-cream.

My sister and I, we can't help looking how she's
holding up the traffic – the drivers,
this honking and hooting male collective
god Alpheus losing his cool,
melting to rivers under the sea from here to the Peloponnese.

Persephone

Our bus drove us past orchards of citrus and loquat
and Enna on a height above us.
It was April, Persephone's month of flowers.

In Catania was a park with a calendar of stones,
daily rearranged with the date. Wedding couples
posing in front of their very own day.

The foreground was a pond, with one white swan
and one black swan. One wrong look,
and that pond could take you right down to Hades.

The Mormons in Sicily

There's something I didn't mention,
that time we stood in the bus going to Monreale
watching the Mormons, noticing their badges
– the title Elder translated "Anziano":
Anziano Norton, Anziano Schmitz, Anziano Miller,
and Anziano Bellini the local boy,
returning from Utah with his brethren
to convert the rest of the island,
perhaps including his mother.
There was great zeal to labour in the vineyard.

What I didn't say was: as the bus filled with people
and jolted uphill to the cathedral
a man, crowded in behind me, was jolting
in a rhythm that wasn't the bouncing suspension,
and for a good ten minutes was fucking me,
without actually fucking me, till the bus
came to his ordinary street and he got off as usual,
while we stayed on to the end of the line,
to enjoy the Norman masterpiece
with the Latter-Day Saints.

Discover London

Say it in the dullness of the afternoon cloud,
say it fresh-hearted as the new laid egg:
there are no discoveries in London.
London is a ship aground in its river,
voyaging through the changes of driftwood,
so each tide it arrives, and it arrives
under all the routine varieties of sunset.

Here are the nine urban moods; the eight entertainments;
the seven choices of all-day breakfast
in every neighbourhood café,
passed by each red bus;
the ten million occasions daily
for someone to notice their own brick wall,
or grab at St Paul's from a train: it's their very own,
but still it's further off than they can hold,
even for a second.

Shoreditch Orchid

They're grubbing up the old modern
rusty concrete lampposts,
with a special orange grab
on a fixture removal unit.
The planters come up behind
with new old lampposts in lamppost green,
and bury each root in a freshly-dug hole.
The bus can't get past, brooding in vibrations.
We're stuck at the half-refurbished
late-Georgian crescent of handbag wholesalers.
The window won't open. The man behind me
whistles "What a Wonderful World",
and I think to myself:

Any day soon
the rubble will be sifted; the streets all swept,
and we'll be aboard a millennium tram ride,
the smooth one we've been promised, with a while yet to go
until the rising sea and the exterminating meteor,
but close before the war
starting with the robocar disaster.
And when the millennium crumbles,
I'll be squinting through the corrugated fence
at the wreck of the mayor's armoured vehicle, upside down
where they dumped the files of the Inner City Partnership;
and as I kick an old kerbstone
I'll find you, Shoreditch orchid, true and shy,
rooting in the meadow streets
through old cable, broken porcelain, rivets and springs;

living off the bones of the railway.
You'll make your entry unannounced,
in the distraction of buddleia throwing its slender legs
out in the air from nothing,
from off the highest parapets, cheap

attention-seeking shrub from somewhere
like nowhere. But here
you'll identify your own private genes,
a quiet specimen-bloom seeded in junk,
and no use to any of us; only an intricate bee-trap
composed in simple waxy petals, waiting
for the bees to reinvent their appetite.

We'll be waiting for the maps to kindle
as we get settled, where we find ourselves
undiscovering the city,
its lost works, disestablished
under the bridges. There's no more bargaining
for melons and good brass buttons.
We share your niche
and crouch as the falling sun
shines through smoke, and the lampposts
fail to light the night to the place all buses go.

Policeman, Stoke Newington

Standing close up to a policeman,
I can get a free look at his
uniform, its unrevealing midnight matt cloth
and silvery buttons, its clever gussets,
and places for his walkie-talkie,
yes, his walkie-talkie tucked under his tunic.
Serious tailoring.

He glances at me sideways,
the expressionless professional
caught in this personal necessity
here at the cash dispenser in the street,
as if performing a secret habit: *Don't be ashamed*,
I could tell him, *It's a normal function, we all do it.*

Satisfied, taking a single circumspect motion
to finish his transaction and reinsert
his wallet in its place, he walks on,
a bobby in a helmet, upright in a naughty world:
he's a policeman with money, stowed
in the safest pocket in the street.

Routemasters

Up at the Common where the buses hang around
the buses are hanging around, red vine tomatoes
in a bunch. Still hanging around, the immortals.

Boys in generations have spotted them. They rattle
through Church Street; or they progress past Selfridges
at the speed of a houseboat, showing off an aptitude for London.

Diamond graffiti windows, mouldy upholstery,
rested each Sunday for a garage sabbath with the engineers.
It can't be long before their definitive retirement.

Through weekdays and Saturdays, wind, rain, sun
and the dull particulate smog of this atmosphere,
drive the blood along our veins, carry us home.

Endeavours

The developing symphony dreams itself into shape
till a rhythmic squealing blunders in, and the orchestra
and audience all stare at the real bedroom in the morning.

Face the dawn's opening phrases, the starling in the trellis
and low sun across the houses. Vapour trails in empty sky
in strokes like a double W, the morning arrivals.

The stripy shirt today. It chooses my mood. I suit it.
The streets are all laid open for the walk to the station.
The trains are full of people who also chose wakefulness.

Off to the endeavours of our lives, submitting to
the truth, or creating it; leading a life of honour
with pen, drill, scalpel, sword, and book of experience.

The others this morning on our derailable transport
share with me this place of dirt and disagreement,
hold it together in between stations, between dreams.

Mr Luczinski Takes a Tram

He has paid a small coin to a glass box
like a fairground machine.

A dull purple ticket
permits him to sway with the tram

which pushes on through a city of breezeblocks
and neo-baroque stucco.

The people might be
his second cousins twice removed:

a woman in fishmonger's gloves
coming home from the market,

a man balancing two dusty old bikes
between fellow-passengers.

In this incarnation, his tweed suit
is not quite threadbare enough.

He hasn't lost his sense of direction but
it has nowhere to take him.

Somewhere at the end of this line
is a field of dandelions and a bluebell wood.

The Monkey
Vladislav Khodasevich

It was hot. Forests were burning. Time
tediously dragging. At the neighbouring dacha
the cockerel crowed. I went out past the gate.
There, propped against the fence, on the bench,
a vagrant was dozing, a Serb, thin and dark.
A cross of heavy silver hung on his
half-naked chest. Drops of sweat
were rolling down him. Up on the fence
a monkey in a red skirt was sitting
greedily chewing the leaves
of the dusty lilacs. Her leather collar
was pulled back by a heavy chain,
catching her throat. The Serb, hearing me,
woke up, wiped off his sweat and asked me
to give him some water. But he barely sipped –
how cold was it? – put a dish on the bench
and at once the monkey, dipping
a finger in the water, seized
the dish in both her hands.
She drank, crouched on all fours,
her elbows leaning on the bench.
Her chin nearly touched the planks,
her backbone arched high above her dark
and balding head. It was the position
Darius must once have taken, bending
at a puddle in the road the day he fled
in front of Alexander's mighty phalanx.
When she had drunk it all, the monkey
swept the dish from the bench, stood up
and – when could I ever forget this moment? –
offered me her black and calloused hand,

still cool from the water, extending it...
I have shaken hands with beauties, poets
and leaders of nations – not one hand displayed
a line of such nobility! Not one hand
has ever touched my hand so like a brother's!
God is my witness, no one has looked at me
so wisely and so deeply in the eye,
indeed into the bottom of my soul.
This animal, destitute, called up in my heart
the sweetness of a deep and ancient legend.
Life in that instant seemed to me complete;
a choir of sea-waves, winds and spheres
was shining and was bursting in my ear
with organ music, thundering, as once
it did in other, immemorial days.
Then the Serb got up, patted a tambourine.
Taking up her seat on his left shoulder
with measured rocking, the monkey rode
like a maharajah on an elephant.
The enormous crimson sun
stripped of its rays
hung in the opalescent smoke. A sultry
thunderlessness covered the feeble wheat.

That was the day of the declaration of war.

7 June 1918, 20 February 1919

Nervous

First identify it, name the condition. Good to know where you are, whether it's contagious.

Establish the context and time frame, a forward view, the prospect of a devastated country.

Distant thunder and a slight change in temperature. A small gust extinguishes your candle.

No need to worry, they assure us all, but sudden mood swings are likely while this continues.

Nervousness, Irritability, Want of Strength, symptoms that occasion your concern.

Fear, Dread, Neuralgia, for instance. Hysteria, Disturbed Sleep, Melancholy. No contest:

Baldwin's Nervous Pills, one and elevenpence ha'penny, post free. Made for just your type of constitution.

Stockpiled at docksides, in sheds on stilts, waiting for the surge in demand, instant consignment.

The other problem, the infectious kind of thing, that may need some further consultation.

Opening the post, watch for the powder leaking. Remember, you must concentrate.

February Charm

It won't be long now, the February struggle
through a plateau of low reserves and cold.
Daylight enough to get home before dark,
enough to see it's the bottom of the end.

The marshes will be water-filled a long time,
maybe in June they still won't be passable.
Years back, I could cross all through those
dry winters – in a good frost, no trouble.

I put a charm into the end of February,
a stake I want to lose. It isn't yet begun,
so never mind the little enchantments
like crocuses the ground has hoarded up:

other plants can struggle all through winter,
and die in March. But the gift – when I stand
one day soon in a patch of old grass and reed
as the caterpillar trainset rattles to Chingford –

that depends on what I give up now, as if
my charm has made the spring; the spring
will release my own little wheel, and the bell
that wakes my effort to believe it's what there is.

The Special

They do exist: they puff and clank into the stations
the old way. Desire for their kind appears inbuilt.

Lining the bridges, beards and binoculars
await the arrival of Napoleon, of Hannibal.

With scarlet-fronted buffers, the beast-machine
rolls on snorting, its breath a chugging nebula.

A boy is lifted on father's shoulder to catch
a moment in a life, a seed-time, an enabling.

Unashamed wonderment in trains, the love
of the moving device, orderly and noble.

City Boy

In a moment of love I caught a sense of money,
and how they make it, and make it up. That city boy,
comfortable and sharp in a suit that fits him,
steers through the station when the city bars have closed,
and an evening of gin is a good anaesthetic
when he trips and smacks the concrete. He'll get home,
he'll recover in the faith that the concrete
is his dream of money: work and lust
made into metal and paper, made into numbers
that whisper to each other, transact and multiply.
Even after closing time, spreadsheets
are building up office blocks, and credit
that creates the pavement to land on.
I saw the drunken city exercise discretion, and
the sober city dream of how to keep it happening.
I watched the city boy get up and walk. I felt how this money
is part of us, and keeps ourselves within it. Some of it
has to be love, what we hope and where we're tender.
All we have is trust for it to care for us, curse us
and keep us in harness, to work for something in a city
made out of buildings and people standing up, or falling down.

Found

Hop. The chalk on the loosening concrete slabs,
marked out for the throw. Skip. Round the block,
skim free on the polished granite. Jump. Turn around
on the spot, chase it, catch it up, catch it: or lose it
into the space opening between the up and the down.

Some days the ticket jams in the slot, some days
a train comes in, caught like a ball in your palm.
Pay your coin for the music that carried you safely
off the wooden escalator. You have a guide,
and down in the filthy tunnels a warm wind pushes you

somewhere inside this earth where you might have come from,
somewhere you don't know – you're living on its outside,
dancing attendance on spinning opportunities, counting
the balls in the air, eyes open for the found penny
– but still you can go further. Come down this way,

there's a thin gap, and a sloping passage descends
into an empty tomb – unfinished, or the rich goods
carted off by the robbers, the connoisseurs, the tourists,
the knowingly undersold: a whole city's turnover,
brought down and squared off in marble corners.

Turn through a long dripping hallway, sideways
into a cavern. The floors are pools, and the walls
are alive under layers of crystal and slime,
luminous worms that shine like pips on a domino.
Here, bedded down in limescale, you find the stone token.

Chip it out, careful not to compromise the patina.
Wrap it, and bring it secretly back up into your life,
the day job oiling and turning the numbered wheel:
working for the right combination to break the bank,
shaking down for the once, the twice, the roll over and out.

The Monkey of Forgetting

A monkey opens the ornamental grating
where the lost toys, papers, forgotten buttons
and rubbish of days have slipped through.

The monkey starts with a will to rummage
in this wreck of my past, and I cringe.
No one should know about what I loved.

The monkey is sniffing things, throwing them at me,
items I never noticed were gone, licking them,
peeing on them. Things I might yet find I needed.

Hard to tell how much he means it to hurt.
Blame it on the monkey's own sense of loss,
the babyhood of clinging to the hard wire breast.

The Captive

Give a small donation, you bastards, ransom
for a prisoner in a kind of box, his body
a kind of harness that grips all round,
his bursting musculature, look, lovely –
here he is, ladies and gents, your applause
for he's eager to please, a rhinoceros in heat,
look at him, give him his freedom, salvation

or something to make him look satisfied,
let him work his way out of those irons,
requited, salved in his weary skin,
give him balm for its chafing,
rancid butter to oil his limbs,
let him growl and whimper for his tea
– but give him his tea when it's time, every
beast deserves respect inside
and you'll give him that, ladies and gentlemen,
worth it to calm his soul

                                                    – your soul,
because if he was you it'd be the same, you're
a captive, your limbs cramped, body disheartened,
home ransacked, inner resources all rinsed out,
but you're ready for a slave's retaliation,
waiting for the moment to reinvest
your two pennyworth into the wreck of yourself,
the price of your other life.

Natural History Museum

I wish Lord let me be nervous again, as confidence makes them wary,
and please make me meek – as if it could make them love me –
but for now I want to shout *Fuck* and my tone may be unsympathetic,
though I don't have the accent for street ranting.

I don't live like that either, I do enjoy a steady job and comforts.

*

I wish to propitiate the Ilford Mammoth.
I'd pray to refashion the instruments of peace,
be famous for it: I'll be dead soon enough
and they say you can't take it with you.
You'll be dead, too, and then you'll be sorry:
we shouldn't throw away our advantages.

Today, I wish to be as unknown as yesterday,
yet never unhappy with my broken trumpet,
even now I know that it's mine:
I grew up thinking it's others that are chosen,
I'm not the one that must break the instrument, then
twist it back into tone.

I wish to kneel at the rail of the exhibit.

*

The Mammoth is depicted walking up the High Road
in front of a double decker bus its own size. I ask
do they do this as a postcard, they suggest I suggest it.

They do a postcard of fleas in Mexican costume.

*

I am moved to set out East, to undertake the sacred journey.
At Seven Sisters I'll buy a ticket for Seven Kings,
to visit the spot where it fell, twisting and trumpeting.
The Borough will have a file on it, there may be a plaque.

I shall keep my feet off the seats, and leave no belongings on the train.

I wish to make the fulfilled pilgrim's return, purged and serene.

Outward

Some account of what is needful.
    First
where we come together:
    paint our chairs and tables
white, and paint our rooms
    with white walls
to face us back
    across to God.
God all round us,
    white and white and white.
Dress in white that shows
    all the dirt from the farm.
For such matter clings to us,
    the undeceiving muck,
the clogging of creation
    wherein we are upheld.
And we must do needlework:
    good plain sewing
for these our white garments
    and undergarments,
white hats, white gloves,
    our white boots, nailed at home.
And there shall be printing
    of the word, in black
on the tough white paper
    rolling from our mill.
Black ink our one thread
    out of the dark,
turning our faces to the light.
    So then we'll run
out of the printhouses,
    out of the farm gates,

out of the hedged-in lanes
        and on, and further
onto the buses, out to be seen
        with the word, in white:
the righteous and visible,
        walking the cities,
out in the cities of the lost.

Excesses of the Prior of Inchcolm
Deposed from office, 1224

A monk is illuminating
aspects of the deadlier sins.
The Prior is much in his mind.
The blue snake twined
round the capital of Pride
follows his long smooth shape.
Something of his in the smirk
of the Scarlet Whore.

The Prior doesn't inspect the work.
He strides freely, he is not afraid
of the hellfires they resentfully
score down for him. Along this road
he will elevate self and soul: to see
his priority shining out beyond
the stony shape of the cloistered island.

At the Forest Pool

There's a fiddler – he's in a village band, but he's more than that.
He can strike up truth, he's honest with his honey tone:
that's his love, but it doesn't get enough of what he wants,
and he can't find the way beyond it with his bow.
So he goes to the woods. The woods are dark and cold,
and it's been snowing but it didn't stay, only the feeling of snow.
He follows the path to the pool near the top of the wood,
where the pine needles are thick and his feet ruffle them.
The pool is unfrozen, a rill trickles into it but doesn't
stir it up, the surface is glassy. He walks up to the pool
and the pool says to him:
                        "This is your last chance.
You don't remember the other chances.
We're losing patience, and you've been losing time.
Don't expect to find your tune like anyone,
tapping a foot and following a line. Pick it up and play it
when the glasses are empty and the night opens the door.
Use your elbow to guide what's there, your love
makes you ready for a harder beginning.
Here's your life in a longer scrape of the bow.
This pool will stay beside you all the time,
but we're leaving you now,
until a deeper visit."

Fountain of Doom

I went down to the fountain
        to take a good look:
but no one was there
        to be my witness and swear
that's where I was,
        and as there was no one to care
I did a deed
        I could still be responsible for.

Into the stone basin
        I threw all I could throw,
and everything sank
        with a sound of sighing and loss,
and out of it bubbles arose
        and a vapour like smoking rubber,
and something gripped
        with a cold catch on my nose.

The fountain began to rise
        and the fish in it drowned;
the spray became sharp
        till it covered my face in blood;
the slime from the drains
        entered my soul like food;
the things I threw in came up,
        and a pale light glowed.

A cracked bell clanked
        and the fountain played its doom
as the ground heaved
        and out of it something sang
like the last note
        charmed from a shrivelling lung,
and all my things
        flew back to my heart to belong.

Crossroads

Through the night, forms of the untoward
come forward in their best clothes, and stink.

They're ordering trains across your life, got you
in mind, singled out when they send in the tanks.

We can hope to face them down, one by one,
each of us earn a road to hell on our own donkey.

A standing stone marks the crossroads where
Cerberus pees three times with his special tincture.

Think of how each of us will join them, given
a part to play, a part of the cold unthinkable.

Years of counting the small curses and blessings,
offerings of resentment, every grunt of thanks.

Through the night, watch and listen as they all move
slowly through you, they rumble a little, they twinkle.

In the Deep

Were you down in the deep
and they had to drag you up
gasping for air in the night,
holding yourself in the grim bucket,
taking the sides with clawing hands
to the top, against the pull on every molecule?

Peace down there
is a slow drip in the dark,
and the creatures have no colour,
no eyes as you think of eyes,
but they have lips and they feel,
they have insides, they have nerves of milk.

Necessary as water, this dark,
and the disappearing into it.
Springs underground trickling
feed the tunnels, they fill where
you swim under the overworld,
underneath Cape Town, Jakarta, Milwaukee.

There are others, unknown,
unidentifiable,
inside the deep, seeking
with fingertips to recognise
from long ago facing you on trains,
on buses, sharing the bumpy old mailcoach.

Once in the open, at Stratford,
I saw a dragonfly enter the train
and my mind had to direct it
out, before the sliding doors
closed on a journey down the tube,
the rest of its life an unprecedented mileage:

a mercy forced upon me
for this airborne life
hatched out of the mud.
My element chooses me.
I let the bucket lift me up
and out from the deep watery murk, my hemlock.

Early

There was the sun that crashed through the silent doorway,
and blue open early morning that pushed past where he stood,
watching: small haloes of colour dragged at the woman
entangled in the chandelier, her hair tugging and trailing.

All that brown and gold in the light, and the dark beads of her dress
crackling as he gently tried to wrench her out of the trap.
She seemed grateful yet angry at having reason to thank him
so she made him invisible, turning to wake him out of her life.

He leapt in his sleep like a deer through bushes but didn't wake
because every thorn on the branches brought back the dark,
and night was still on the black side of the waiting moon
impatient to get lost, to push him back in, back in.

Vexation

Though the ice is miles thick, underneath
are tropical fossils, snug in their clay.
Base camp has all your needs. Why leave it?
Fix the equipment and go, nevertheless.
    Because there's work to be done,
    and the world isn't ready.

There's the lonely captain, so disciplined,
anything losable attached to him by a lanyard,
yet he's lost it. Half castaway, half Nelson,
he still has the fogs, the pebbles and surf.
    Because there's work to be done,
    and it's his responsibility.

As the good book suggests, the figs don't give
a damn about Jesus, they just aren't coming.
The vicar can marry a vixen: it's a fact,
the grapes are going to vinegar.
    Because there's work to be done,
    and only the laws of physics to do it.

So: baptise me wading in that minor estuary
and let the wind dry me all across the wide beach.
You'll have to drown me in what I take for granted,
inoculate me with death: then you can put me to work.
    Because there's work to be done
    and the world still isn't ready.

Kings

The king of touch is good to fling with, waltzing
from ballroom to bedroom. Feel under his skin,
the veins his blood is roaring through.

You can't leave them there,
dancing on the edge of a cliff.

The king of tact knows a trick you don't,
but he holds his powers in reserve, his
is the unexpected gift.

Sometimes heroism makes good sense
though you can't insist on it.

The king of trust is aware what the night can be,
and he waits there, sparking and vulnerable, till
he can prick a hole in the dark.

"Take off that ridiculous gown," he says.

The kings of truth have told you: "People go, they die,
they won't be perfect. Don't wait up for your climbing joy."

Sweat is water, salt and grease.

Housework

Sometime like the middle Wednesday in August
you might understand what it was that you needed,
undutiful steward of what you intended:
retitling and annotating it,
haunted by the one good idea,
handed more to do by the buckets and brooms.

When the day has come for our dead reckoning,
undoubted evidence of the thought and its deed,
untidy dishes and old ends of the truth,
noted ingratitudes, and
unsubtle distinctions of tone:
we'll be glad of our dirt then, for the buckets and brooms.

I don't want to have to invent the only antidote:
I spend time on indiscriminate devilment.
I'll find my mind undusted
in the teeth of disaster,
I'll find procrastination its own reward,
I'll find the buckets and brooms, the buckets and brooms, the buckets

Done

And when the time is full, the space will empty,
sorting its cards and working through the suits,
aces to kings, a line they can fall into.
Glasses poured resourcefully will toast
the wine they finish, as the fugue at last
comes in for landing at its place of safety.
Nothing remains to do but find the best
exit, the weighty door that closes lightly.

On the table, work and food that stand
for food and work, their heart-caressing fact,
their apt and subtle-tasting nourishments.

Day will be opened by a bird's exact
and confident call; the night's own ignorance
fetches a star, and wakes with time in hand.

Therese

Gottfried Keller

You baby-faced boy,
how deep is that stare?
What did your eyes ask me
with that unspoken dare?

The aldermen of the town,
all the great and the wise,
are standing dumbfounded
at what you ask with your eyes.

There's a seashell you'll find
on my big sister's shelf:
hold it up to your ear now,
you'll answer yourself.

St Katharine's Dock

In clear brown water you can make out fish
clustering in groups, four or five abreast.

A sky full of helicopters, and behind them
airliners, they bring importance, trade, prosperity.

Sacks and planks on the wharfside, loaded
and unloaded. Smoke and tar flattening the breeze.

The docks refurbished with cafés and shops:
cocktail dresses, flowers, marzipan, porcelain.

Three hundred yards from here my great grandmother
lived in a tenement a step from the poorhouse.

Rusty freighters from the Baltic or the Black Sea;
businessmen for lunch, from Paris and Brussels.

Refugees from pogroms, eight to a room.
Little black fishes gathering round the piers.

Tchotchkes

Living room: three cubist prints above the day-bed;
the headscarfed woman who nods and sways;
two Israeli figures in costume. A photo of my father
at my age now. We aren't quite sure why this one.

Kitchen: French coffee grinder, blue enamel casserole,
the ingenious parsley mill; set of Hebrew alphabet
fridge magnets (recent).

Study: on the filing cabinet (research on Jewish music)
one candlestick, a Russian nesting doll,
a revolving plastic Roof with its Fiddler.

The doll opens up for two generations,
then one more, blank and unforthcoming.
The Fiddler chimes a tune I don't recognise,
deeply sad and Yiddish. It keeps turning and playing,
one of those day-before-yesterday tunes
that come in unannounced.
I leave it where it is.

I go back for it.

Family

I'm getting used to the household here,
"informal", I think you said.
But who is the woman that brings rice puddings
and tucks you up in bed?

"I thought you might ask, and it's hard to explain,
but let me think this out:
she's my ex-lover's ex-lover's ex-lover's mother,
she likes to get out and about."

On Tuesday I met with a man on the stairs,
he was holding up a length of pipe.
He ruffled his moustache as he gave me a smile
– do you think I'd be his type?

"That's my ex-lover's ex-lover's therapist's plumber,
he came to fix the U-bend and stayed.
He's always handy with his monkey wrench
but he's not to be had, I'm afraid."

Who was the man that called last night?
When I told you, you grabbed at the phone.
He was obviously someone special to you
so I thought I'd leave you alone.

"He's my three-times-ex-lover's next lover's lover,
we go back quite a long way.
We may not ever have been that close
but we're family, I think you'd say.

"We've often bumped into each other in crowds
– once we met at a bus stop in Spain –
but he's dying now, at his parents' house.
I'll never see him again."

Hunger

Eating has been leaving me hollow
for a man born creating
new appetites, raising desires.
He's always leaving
unfinished business, reaching
for more than one requiring
more of him. Watch him building
a naked art form, letting it lift. Gulping
it in. A need the size of Glasgow

but London-greedy. Yes, you. Mouth full
of native tongue, but you make yourself
understood. When it arises, we hold it
how it comes, how we like it. But
it's holding only a snatched handful
of days from a year and both of us
insatiable – better put it away.
It's getting impossible. Let's give it up.

I walk home cold at midnight, past the baker's:
breathe in the cloud of warm yeast, growing itself.

Liverpool St

Meeting at unappointed times, crossing the marble floors
of the refurbished terminus, we celebrate with food, choosing
station pastries or cartons of burger-fries; and we talk
on the train, or sometimes we don't; sometimes that matters,
for reasons of living together, making our way home.

Tonight on the five-forty-five, the couple sitting opposite
get working on separate crosswords like in-trays of invoices,
till one anagram calls out for the full attention of two;
and silently they distribute all of the concatenations,
finding between them the unspoken words to balance the clues.

Catching up with each other halfway to where we're going
any day is a possibility; and an unexpected extra.
We meet in a station, or we coincide in the bathroom,
we cross and merge in parallels less than a pillow apart:
joined-up people, finding the world as wide as our bed.

Fragment 105a
Sappho

It's like the sweet apple reddening
    at the top of the twig,
the one at the tip, the topmost,
    that the apple-pickers neglected
though they haven't actually forgotten it
    – they just weren't quite able to get at it.

Splendour

At any given point they balance:
opportunity and
        disaster.

              For instance they collide
browsing at the supermarket,
        fondling fat-nippled lemons.
They fill up the trolley
        with cartons of ass's milk,
– it's organic – take it home
and try it in the shower:
a new cheese is born.

            Another time, they meet
in the empty library, looking for
a mystery in the stacks, guesswork
and trial and error but
niftily shuffling the catalogue
        they've cracked it, Proust in a haiku.

           They've got the formula,
they set off the reactions.
One has a trigger finger holding
back, against its nature,

                the other has a gun
ready to blast the whole plantation
out of orbit
into a new story of dark light,
a force to separate
        the waters from the firmament.

                    The sun rises over
a half-destroyed city. One of them's blind,
the other's deaf – now how will they get across
what makes them
            responsible together
for the splendour of this dawn,
                and the birdsong?

Birdsong

Words that are nothing but breath of centuries,
spoken for food, prayer, sex, the jargons of craft;
and hand signals, handshakes, nods and winks,
fashion statements, courtship dances:

all that vocabulary. Why don't we just
put our beaks together and blow?
Berkeley Square on a rainy night,
wet trees to sweeten the notes of a trill.

The Forge

Iron smelted in the furnace, poured out
and moulded as a ploughshare: the thing
the forge dreams up, and a fresh pond to cool it.

In their time, they'll be called to this place
by the true anvil bell, and take their mandate
each with aching lips touched by a burning coal.

They'll come out with prophecies like blades.
The blacksmith has overhauled their wagons,
I'll watch them lining up for the great crossing,

the pilgrimage: a purer traffic, a longer
trail through the distance, the mountains
glistening like crystal when they think of them.

Offer what they bargained for, outcomes of their toil,
their wish-lists and votive offerings, grant them
a portion of the earth's crust to harvest,

but hold me off from visions and touchings,
your slivers of life, your phials of spirit.
I might yet continue along this furrow for ever.